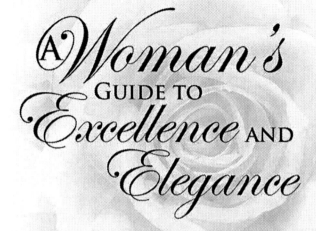

A Woman's Guide to Excellence and Elegance

PATRICE M. ELLIS

Xulon PRESS

A Woman's Guide to Excellence and Elegance
by Patrice M. Ellis

Printed in the United States of America

ISBN-13: 978-1-60034-951-5
ISBN-10: 1-60034-951-X

Cover Design & Layout by:
Joanne Nicolls
www.creationdesignsgroup.com

Proofreading by:
Yvette Farrington

Cover Photography by:
Keith Oliver Dawkins

www.xulonpress.com

Foreword

Just a little over 20 years ago, I stepped into one of the greatest seasons of my life. That season commenced with my meeting and developing a personal relationship with Patrice. What initially attracted me to her was her unique personal display of deportment that was sealed with elegance and steeped in excellence.

I believe that this work Patrice has put into print is extremely effective and powerful. Not necessarily because of the information, which I am sure will positively contribute to the personal development of the women who will read it, but primarily because it's an outflow of her life's experience. And I can say without reservation or hesitation that Patrice is a godly example of elegance and style, internally and externally. Even heaven must be proud. Indeed, she represents the Kingdom well!

I commend my dear wife and life's partner for her sensitivity and for her appreciation of the gift that God has placed in her to share with women around the world who wish to have a testimony of elegance and operate in excellence.

Happy Reading,
BISHOP NEIL C. ELLIS

TABLE OF CONTENTS

INTRODUCTION

*W*oman: what an intelligent piece of workmanship! Made out of the rib of a man and named by the flesh out of whom she came. There hasn't been another piece of handiwork like this since.

Can't you see then how very special you are? God formed you and fashioned you to be beautiful, tender, and wonderful to look at. Something to be admired, desired and inspired; a showpiece.

Yes, this book is designed to get you to the point of becoming inspired to be the woman God has called you to be in grace, charm, poise and elegance.

Proverbs 31:30 says, "Charm is deceitful and beauty is passing, but a woman who fears the Lord shall be praised." Above all else, along with our beauty, our charm, our poise, our elegance and our grace, we ought to be women who fear God and love Him with all our hearts.

May this work that God has mandated me to write not only be a blessing to you, but my prayer is that it also propels you to a point of 'excellence and elegance' in your walk with HIM.

PART ONE

HOW TO STAY FRESH WHEN YOU HAVE A LONG DAY

All of us have long days at some point, especially us as women, because of the multiple roles that we have to facilitate.

It is sometimes difficult to leave work and go home to change, so we have to go straight to the next event.

Here are a few tips to keep you smelling fresh and still feeling confident:

1. Take a good shower / bath in the morning.

2. When purchasing your favorite fragrance, be sure to invest in the whole bath line if it is available.

3. After taking your shower, layer with lotion or body cream. Apply your fragrance not just to your skin, but also hold the fragrance about 12 inches away, and spray your garments.

4. Spray fragrance to pulse points i.e. behind your ear, behind your knees, in your groin, the inner part of your elbow etc.

5. Shaving under your arm and pubic area helps, because hair traps odor.

6. You can also apply (poo) oil or any fragranced oil to your groin and pubic area.

7. Wear a panty shield and take along an extra one.

8. Sprinkle the panty shield with 'Ammens' powder or some feminine powder, or spray the panty shield with some feminine deodorant spray.

9. Wear clean underwear at all times, including bras. (I know that all of us have our favorites).

10. Put a cotton ball sprayed with the fragrance you're wearing in the front section of your bra where the two cups meet.

11. A light touch-up with the fragrance during the day works.

12. Choose deodorant based on effectiveness, not popularity.

13. It's also important that you test the effectiveness of the fragrance that you are wearing with your body chemistry, not popularity. E.g. if after a long day without touching up with the fragrance, compliments are still given, this might be suggestive of effectiveness.

14. Do not wear pantyhose repeatedly without washing them.

15. Don't forget to take along toothpaste and toothbrush.

16. Lightly freshen up your makeup at the end of the day.

17. Take an extra pair of pantyhose for later, if possible.

18. Make sure that your shoes are clean and presentable.

SO YOU HAVE LOTS OF CLOTHES, BUT NOTHING TO WEAR?

For some of us, a closet is a very small cramped place where everything is smashed together.

We can rarely find what we need. When we finally locate something to wear, we're not always pleased, and wonder if it makes us look our best.

The next few pages teach us how to decide what clothes are worth investing in, and show ways to dress for comfort, work, play and evening. It will also teach us how to build a wardrobe that will last.

WHAT FITS ME?

The colour of one's outfit might be perfect, the pattern and the texture of the material may be pure genius, but if the lines of an outfit are off and it doesn't fit properly, you might as well start over.

- Be careful of sales persons encouraging you to purchase something that you really do not want or that you do not look good in. For them it might simply be about making a sale.

- Until or unless you are comfortable with how the attire fits, do not purchase.

⤜⦾⦿⦾⤛

WHAT TO WEAR

1. If you are big (pleasantly plump), **Do Not** wear big clothes. It makes you look bigger. Acknowledge that you are the size that you are. If you think that you have on too much weight, get rid of the pounds, but don't try to dress as if they are not there.

2. If your blouse (top) is full, then the bottom should be closer fitting and vice versa.

3. Dark colours make you look slimmer.

4. If you have broad hips, **Do Not** wear tops that stop at the widest part of your hips.

5. **Do Not** wear anything with a drawstring waist if you are broad (full-figured).

6. No pleats or gathers if you're broad (wide) across the hips.

7. If you are short, **Do Not** wear anything with cuffs.

8. **Do Not** wear wide legged pants unless it is flowy material.

9. **Do Not** wear A-lined garments if you are short.

10. Short people should not wear clothes with large patterns.

11. **If You Are Heavy Busted**:

    (a) Wear tailored clothing.

    (b) Wear high-neck lined and below the waist length tops.

(c)   Wear dark colours on top.

(d)   **Do Not** wear tops with large patterns.

(e)   **Do Not** wear ruffles.

12.   If wearing strappy stuff, wear broad (wide) straps.

13.   Smaller busted people should wear lighter colours on top.

14.   **Do Not** wear a whole denim outfit to work.

15.   **Do Not** wear floral pants to work.

16.   **Do Not** wear anything that's too tight, too loose or too bleached out at work.

17.   Don't be a slave to size. Buy what fits.

CHECKPOINTS TO DETERMINE PROPER FIT

1.   If your blouse pulls at the buttons, it's too tight.

2.   Check for puckering along the seams.

3.   Pleats should lie flat (pants, skirts, dresses, etc.) and not pull apart.

4.   Long sleeved clothing should extend down to wrist joint.

5.   Zippers should lie flat and be easy to use.

6.   Stripes should hang properly.

7.   Do you have extra fabric around the hips of a skirt, pants or jacket?

8. Make sure no threads are hanging.

9. No panty lines should show (this could mean that clothes are too tight).

10. No blouse tail should be showing through skirts or pants except when there is a jacket.

11. Make sure there are no extra creases when you iron your clothes (particularly on your pants).

12. No hanger marks are visible on your pants.

Wearing clothes well is about posture. There is only so much a beautiful jacket can do; the rest is up to you.

⁓⌁⌁⌁⁓

UNDERWEAR

Even though your underwear is hidden from the naked eye, it should not be underestimated.

1. Start to build a basic underwear wardrobe with basic colors: black, white, nude etc.

2. Fit and fabric make all the difference.

3. Spend time finding the right size and cut.

4. Make sure leg holes and waist do not cut into your body.

5. Think about the usage. Underwear that looks the prettiest on its own often looks lumpy under your clothes.

6. Make sure your panty has a cotton crotch.

7.   Make sure that your panty is your size.

8.   Wear thongs only if they are suitable for you as they can be pretty uncomfortable.

9.   Make sure your undergarment has a support for your type of figure and can control the jiggles.

10. Check out the lingerie store, and speak with experts in the field to identify body slimmers that are necessary for your figure type.

This is not about changing yourself to make you look like something you're not, but it's about slimming, comfort for sleeping, and making the best out of what you already have.

಼ೲ⊚ග֊಄

BATHING SUITS

Most of us won't mind looking like those women in the 'Sports Illustrated' magazines, but the reality is, most of us need some kind of help. Know your body type and your trouble spots.

Do you have big hips and a small chest? Is your tummy thicker than you would want it to be? Are you self-conscious about your bust?

Try on a range of styles and choose a pattern to camouflage specific areas.

WHAT'S IN MY CLOSET?

STORING

Storing shoes in boxes allows you to pile them up on a shelf instead of losing them on the closet floor. For a quick view:

• Label the boxes with a Polaroid picture.

• Write the colour on the box.

• Create your stacks in colour code.

• Create your stacks in categories, i.e. church shoes, work shoes, casuals, etc.

• Slit the top of the shoe box a few times for ventilation.

Consider giving your stuff a shelf life. If you seem to never wear it, apply a twelve month cycle, and if you haven't worn it in a year, then give it away.

ORGANIZE

1. Re-design your closet so you can see everything.

2. Group things either by size, colour, types, i.e. blouses, skirts, etc. and organize those by colour and type code.

3. Put all of your casuals together, all work clothes together, etc.

4. Get closet organizers to create space.

5. Group blouses by sleeve types, e.g.: long, short, sleeveless or by fabric type.

INVESTMENT GUIDES

- Buy fewer but better quality things.

- Buy things that are timeless in colour, cut and pattern.

- Consider how you feel in the outfit.

- How often will you wear it?

- Invest in a beautifully tailored suit and blazer.

- Invest in a high quality pants in a neutral colour and the perfect black dress.

- Consider if this is simply a fad.

- Purchase a few T-shirts.

- Purchase a few designer jeans.

- Purchase a few casual summer dresses.

- Invest in suede shoes.

- Ask yourself, "Does this compliment my size, shape or age?"

- How much should I spend?

- Organize your budget.

- Sort out what you want from what you need, then think about what you can afford.

- Money well spent will buy you high quality fabric, sensible design and remarkable workmanship e.g. a black, exquisite leather bag you will probably have for years. It's the loud-colored purse that might be a waste of your money.

- Invest in a good basic wardrobe and spruce it up with a few things every season. This will enhance what you already own.

No matter what you wear for whatever occasion, before you step out of your home be certain that it's:

(a) Appropriate

(b) Confidence Boosting

(c) Psychologically Comfortable

(d) Your shoes are in good condition, i.e. heels aren't scuffed; heel & sole are intact and are nicely polished.

(e) Also check the sheerness of your garment. Stand in the doorway, spread your legs apart, and look down between your legs and see if you can see straight through your garment. If you can, and it is daylight, be careful and know that others would be able to see through your legs as well.

Examine yourself in the mirror and look for signs of imperfections: hems, cuffs, buttons, button holes, hanger marks, zippers, seams, snaps, hook & eyes, collars. Ensure that no threads are hanging and your clothes aren't torn in any way.

You cannot escape it. High maintenance clothes are like high maintenance relationships. They need a lot of attention. So before purchasing it, ask yourself these questions:

- How delicate is it?

- Does it stain easily?

- How careful do I need to be while wearing it?

- Does it have to be dry-cleaned?

- Does it have to be hand-washed?

- Does it have to be ironed?

- Is it something that you will only wear on special occasions? If yes, then you might want to opt for something that's easier to maintain.

- If no, then you might want to get it.

PART
TWO

COLOURS & THEIR USAGE

The right choice of colour for clothing can be an amazing thing. Most of us do not realize or are not aware of which colours are best for us. Each person's skin and hair are optimally complemented by certain colours. Colours are useful to keep in mind when building a wardrobe. Test a colour against your skin. Does it clarify or smooth your complexion? Does it bring a healthier glow to your face? If so, it's your colour.

BEIGE:

• It never makes a fuss; it's easy to work with.

• It stays neutral.

• It camouflages.

• It shows dirt and wrinkles easily.

• It's not slimming.

• When put together with similar tones, it creates an elongated line.

• Always buy as a suit (pants or skirt) because beiges are hard to match.

• Pearls, gold and shell jewelry work well with beige.

• Suitable for mild climate. In cold winters it works better as an accent.

- Alligator (bag), fake or real, adds a rich texture to basic beige.

- Deconstruct the beige suit and mix with colorful sweaters, blazers, pants or skirts.

- Both black and brown accessories work well with beige.

- Khakis are a reliable, inexpensive classic.

- Colorful stripes play well with khakis.

NAVY:

- Goes well with everything (except navy)

- Serious and sophisticated

- Mixes well with other colours

- Black dresses up navy (e.g. shoes)

- Brown makes navy more casual

- Always buy as a suit (pants/skirt)

- Navy blazer and a navy and white striped shirt is a classic nautical look

- Brightly coloured jeans (lime, pink, white) get instant respectability when paired with a navy blazer

- Camel and gray are two other wardrobe neutrals that compliment navy.

BLACK:

- Hides stains

- Distracts from poor tailoring and general wear

- Goes with all colours

- Looks decent even in the cheapest fabric

- It dresses up

- It dresses down

- Can be elegant, classic, sexy and mournful

- Can go summer or winter

- It stands out, blends in and seduces

- What other colour does all this and takes off pounds

- Opaque black stockings are slimming (tights, thick) and make short hemlines appear longer

- Gold jewelry on black is more elegant (uptown)

- Silver jewelry on black has a little more attitude (is more downtown)

WHITE:

- Commands attention

- Versatile

- Cool looking

- Crisp

- The very lightness of white's purity has made it the colour of heavenly joy and or chastity

- A wardrobe necessity

STRIPES:

- Horizontal (running across) seem more nautical

- Vertical (running up and down) seem more businesslike

- Do not cover yourself in stripes

- They are tiring to the eyes

- Vertical stripes make you look taller

- Horizontal stripes make you look wider and shorter

POLKA DOTS:

- Best used sparingly

- Best on silk scarves

- Comical when they are too large

- Demure when tiny

PLAIDS:

- Best used as accents e.g. scarves, flannel skirts or the lining of a coat

PART
THREE

꙳ꙮ꙳

NECKLINES

Necklines are an important element of your garment. There are numerous necklines, ranging from high to scoop. It depends on whether you want to accentuate your look to provide the pizzazz, or simply make your neckline more comfortable. Some necklines that could add pizzazz or enhance your clothing (especially if you are heavy-chested) are:

- Scoop-neckline

- U-neckline

- V-neckline

These necklines can work for either the well endowed or those who are comfortably proportioned. A special tip for the well-endowed ladies would be:

- Wear a good underwire bra

- Do not wear dresses or blouses that are up to the neck. Of course, you should always be sure that your neckline is modest.

HEMLINES

- Should be either above the knee or below the knee, but never at the knee.

- For evening gowns, your hemlines should be floor length or right above the ankle.

MIXING & MATCHING

- Mixing is not about having a lot of clothes. It's about being resourceful.

- It allows you to create the maximum wardrobe with minimum investment.

- Start with a solid wardrobe of quality basics that are predominantly around a single colour.

- Deconstruct a suit.

- Wear the jacket with other skirts and pants.

- Do the same with the bottom components.

- Mix unexpected colours.

- A blazer with a T-shirt has a whole different personality than one worn with a blouse.

- Ensure that your fabrics blend.

- When I have few items of clothing, I manage better than when I have a lot, because I use my imagination.

- Anything you wear a lot, no matter how pricey, will get cheaper every time you wear it.

❧

CONSIDERATIONS WHEN ATTENDING A WEDDING
(NOT YOURS)

1. Where is the wedding being held (Country)?

2. Venue of the wedding (Church, Garden, Hall or Ballroom).

3. Time of day.

4. Age of the Bride and Groom

5. Whether the couple is hosting the wedding or their parents.

6. The bridal couple's taste & spirit (conservative or far out)

7. Is this the Bride's first marriage?

DAYTIME WEDDING:

1. Short (right above the knee), knee length or mid-calf hemlines, unless the invitation says formal.

2.   No heavy jewelry.

3.   Pants can be worn. Preferably a suit, but something soft and dressy; can also be a 'tux' pants suit.

EVENING WEDDING:

1.   Ankle lengths are preferred.

2.   If the skirt is short, the hemline should be knee length and it should be a tuxedo suit; no short skirt ones.

3.   Sequins jewelry.

4.   Dressy day-wears combined with evening-wear. e.g. lacy shell with a taffeta ball skirt.

5.   Wear floral prints only if they are evening fabric e.g. taffeta, silk or satin.

6.   **DO NOT** wear linen or cotton florals.

7.   Remember, the fancier the event, the smaller the bag should be.

NOTE

*   *No matter what time of day the wedding is, you should not wear an outfit that you wear at work, neither should you wear plain working pumps.*

*   *Never wear <u>white</u> or <u>beige</u> at a wedding. It's an insult to the Bride.*

PACKING

Most people are privileged and blessed to be able to take a vacation or trip once in awhile for a few days.

Unless you are well traveled or a frequent traveler, most of us make the mistake of packing more than we need.

- Your suitcase is your closet when you travel.

- Hard sided luggage prevents wrinkling and protects clothes better.

- Placing folded dress clothes in plastic bags helps to eliminate wrinkles.

THINGS TO THINK ABOUT WHEN PACKING

- How much space does it take up?

- Does it match with other pieces you are taking?

- Will it go for day and evening?

- Can you wash it by hand?

- Can you wear it more than once?

- Does it wrinkle easily?

- How many accessories do you need to take?

- Suit fabric should be seasonless. Ideal travel fabric should bounce back after being crushed.

- They include lightweight wool, crepes or knits, denim, synthetics and synthetic blends.

- Dark colors also don't show dirt as easily as light ones.

- After you've packed the items you need, throw in a few garments and accessories that will help to create varying looks with the clothes you have chosen.

- Travel with a minimal amount of jewelry and always as a carry on.

- Pack a top that can stand on its own without the suit jacket.

- Jeans are comfortable and seasonless, resistant to wrinkling and dirt, and can be dressed up with a blazer.

- Wearing the suit jacket while traveling means that this is less to pack and gives you a look of respectability.

PART
FOUR

BASIC EATING ETIQUETTE & TABLE MANNERS

Most people are embarrassed and feel totally inadequate in this area. Most of their embarassing moments have taken place while dining because they simply do not know any better.

USING BASIC FLATWARE

- Silverware is used from the outside in. Always work your way inward toward the plate.

- A fork or spoon is held between the fore-finger and the middle finger.

- When cutting, hold the fork in your left hand and the knife in your right; each with an index finger pressing down on the handle.

- Cut one piece of food at a time.

- *American style:* transfer fork to right hand, place knife back on plate. Food towards the inside of the fork.

- *European style:* keep fork in left and knife in right hand; food on the back of the fork.

SOUP SPOON

- Soup should be poured into the mouth from the side of an oval soup spoon. Drag the spoon away from you to the edge of the bowl. Rest the spoon on the edge for a moment, then pour the soup.

SILVERWARE PLACEMENT WHEN FINISHED EATING

- Place knife and fork in the 10:20 position or 11:25. Handles to the right (knife blade inward)

- Soup spoon to the right of the soup bowl on the service plate.

- Salad fork and knife: place fork face down in salad bowl on the service plate.

GLASSES

STEMMED GLASSES

- Large (for water)

- Medium (for red wine, cider)

- Small (for white wine)

UNSTEMMED GLASSES

- Short (for juice)

- Tall (mixed drinks non-alcoholic, milk, soda)

STEMWARE

- Cold drinks (hold by the stem)

- Room temperature (grasp the glass at the bottom of its bowl)

STRAWS

- Always pick up the glass when preparing to draw liquid from the straw

NAPKIN

- Place it in your chair if you are returning

- On the table if not returning

- Soil side down on the table

- Gently pat your mouth when finished then place on the right of your plate

꩜

FOOD TRAPS
(HOW TO EAT CERTAIN FOODS)

Ever asked the question, "How do I eat this? Or, "What is the proper way?" Well, here we go...

1.   Bacon

If it's crisp you can eat it with your fingers, otherwise use a knife and fork.

2.   Cake

If it is bite size, feel free to eat it with your fingers.

If it has sauce or is sticky or is served with ice cream, then by all means use a fork and spoon with the fork serving as a pusher and the spoon as a scoop.

3.   Celery Sticks/Pickles

These should be taken off the serving dish with your fingers and placed on your plate to be eaten with your fingers.

4.   Spinach Dip & Chips

Your spinach dip should be taken from the container with a spoon or fork and placed on a plate along with the salsa and/or other side orders. Eating takes place with your fingers.

5.   Chicken

Should be eaten with a knife and fork unless you are at a picnic.

6.   Pasta

Depending on the size, they can be eaten with a fork, e.g. penne, ziti, etc. otherwise you can feel free to eat it by twirling it with a fork. <u>Please</u> do not cut the spaghetti strands with your knife.

7.   Grapefruit Halves

Should be sectioned to make meat more accessible. Sprinkle a little sugar on it (optional) and eat the sections with a spoon.

8.   Oranges/Tangerines

Can be peeled with a knife or fingers. If sectioned or plugged, can be eaten with your fingers, but with a fork if it is served on a plate.

9.   Lemon Wedges

Can be picked up with a fork and then squeezed with the other hand. If you are not using a fork, use your other hand as a shield so as not to squirt the juice on the persons sitting next to you.

10.   Pineapple

Eat with a spoon when cut into bite sizes and with a fork if sliced.

11. **Avocado**

If eating it from the shell, can be eaten with a spoon, however use a fork if cut in pieces.

12. **Cherries/Berries**

If there are no stems use a spoon, otherwise hold the berry by the stem and take one or two bites.

13. **Bread**

Should be torn - not in half, but in one portion of two or three bites at a time, buttered and eaten.

14. **Corn On The Cob**

Should be eaten in an orderly fashion (straight across).

15. **Baked Potato**

Cut the potato in half (lengthwise) push the potato inward from both ends and use a fork to mash in the butter and sour cream, then season to taste.

16. **Cakes and Pies**

Cakes and pies require a fork.

Covered desserts require a spoon (peach cobbler, ice cream, etc.)

17. **Dips**

One dip only (no seconds after biting the item; unless you have your own dip.)

18.   Gum

A polite person will never be seen at a dinner table chewing gum.

◦~◦✿◦~◦

RESTAURANT DINING

THE PROFFERED CHAIR

- This is pulled for the lady. If done in a restaurant, it does not matter if a waiter or waitress pulls it.

ORDERING FROM THE MENU

- Guest should always order from the middle of the menu.

- Never order the cheapest item unless it's just irresistible.

- Never order the most expensive item unless the host announces that the item is fabulous, you must try it and then he orders it for himself or herself.

- Do not mention the financial circumstances of the hosts.

REFUSING DRINK

- Symbolic use of the table setting, turn the appropriate glass down.

- I won't be having wine.

- "Regular or decaf?" "Neither, thank you."

DEPARTING

- Host or guest could suggest that it's time to go.

- Host: "Would you like anything else?" Guest: "Oh no, thank you. This has been delightful."

CHECK GRABBING

- Permissible occasionally.

- Ask the waiter before hand to bring the cheque to you.

BEFORE DINNER

- Don't arrive late but call if there is an emergency and state your approximate time of arrival.

- If you are really hungry before the function, eat a piece of fruit or other snacks before hand so that it doesn't appear that you were starving.

- Only a very close friend of the host should offer to help.

- Do not converse with the wait staff if you know them.

- Hello or good evening is acceptable.

- Conversation can be done afterward, after dinner and away from the table.

TOASTS

- If you are being toasted to, quietly sit there. Afterward, say, "Thank you." Simply pick up a wine or water glass and gesture, then wait until everyone has sipped to the toast. Do not sip from your glass if you are being toasted to.

- Do not read your toast. If it's too long to commit to memory, forget it.

- Keep your toast short (approx. 1 minute.)

SERVING YOURSELF

- Pick up the bowl and offer it to the person on your left; then to the right. Then serve yourself and pass the bowl to your right.

CLEANING YOUR PLATE

- Do not soak up gravy or sauce with bread.

- Do not try to get the last morsel off your plate and into your mouth.

- Your plate should not look like it has been washed.

- It is always proper to leave a bite or two on your plate.

DROPPED NAPKIN

- At a private residence, pick up the napkin. You may continue using it, or ask for another.

- At a restaurant, ask for a replacement.

SILVERWARE DROPPED ON FLOOR

- Always ask for a replacement.

- Do not bend down to search for the lost utensil.

SPILLED DRINK OR FOOD

- Do not create a scene.

- Simply make an apology.

- Allow the host/hostess to clean up the mess.

- Do not try to clean up the mess (havoc's created when everyone tries to help).

- If at a private residence, offer to send the tablecloth to the cleaners. Then pick it up later and return it as soon as possible to the host/hostess.

ELBOWS/HANDS

•   On the table between courses or after the table is cleared.

•   Otherwise, keep arms in your lap.

∾༺ઉ༻∾

SOLUTIONS TO COMMON BLUNDERS

DO NOT	DO
Pick your teeth with toothpick or tine of fork	*Use your tongue discreetly to dislodge food from your teeth or excuse yourself to take care of the problem*
Push food onto your fork with your fingers	*Use your knife to push food onto the fork*
Clean your teeth with your napkin	*Go to the powder room; teeth should never be cleaned in public*

SOLUTIONS TO COMMON BLUNDERS

DO NOT	DO
Blow your nose in a napkin	*Dab your nose discreetly if it bothers you, then excuse yourself to solve the problem if it persists*
Talk with your mouth full	*If asked a question while your mouth is full, clear and swallow before answering*
Reach across the table for an item	*Ask to have it passed to you*
Start eating just as you get your plate	*Wait for everyone at the table to receive their plate, then begin*
Converse with just the person on one side of you	*Try to give them both your attention at intervals*
Suck or lick your fingers at the table	*Wipe it with a napkin otherwise always use knife and fork*

SOLUTIONS TO COMMON BLUNDERS

DO NOT	DO
Burp out loud	Cover your mouth with a napkin to stifle the sound
Order items that are unfamiliar	Ask for interpretation
Say you dislike a food that's being served	Say nothing critical, decline with a smile and say, "No, thank you"
Carry on if you find a foreign matter in the food	Either don't eat the food or ask for a new serving
Spit out a fish or chicken bone directly on the plate	Put it on the fork and then discard it on your plate to the left of food you're eating
Freshen up your lipstick or comb your hair at the table	Go to the powder room
Put your keys, purses, eyeglasses or eyeglasses case, etc. on the table	Keep them in your lap or on a chair next to you if you can

MORE 'NO NOS'

- Do not put salt or any other seasoning on your food before you taste it. This particularly is offensive when dining at someone's residence.

- Don't push your plate away and don't push your chair back when you have finished eating.

- Never pass food to the left, only offer.

- Don't ask people where they are going when they leave the table.

- If you belch say, "Excuse me" to no one in particular.

- Never speak with food in your mouth.

- Never crumble crackers or bread in your soup.

- Never chew ice at the table.

- Never put butter directly on the bread; put butter first on your bread plate or dinner plate.

- Never tilt your chair.

- If someone at the table takes a pill, don't ask what it's for. If you must take medication at the table, don't comment about it. No explanations are necessary.

- Once you pick up a piece of silverware, it never touches the table again. Put your knife and fork right on your plate when not in use.

- The coffee/tea spoon goes **in** the saucer beside the cup.

- If someone uses your bread plate use the side of your dinner plate for your bread.

PART
FIVE

THE RIGHT THINGS TO SAY

A lot of people mean well and generally have good intentions. It is their desire to be friendly and accommodating, but there are people who simply do not know what to say. They always seem to put their foot in their mouth. Are you one of these people? Here's some help:

SYMPATHY

DO NOT SAY	DO SAY
Things could be worse	*I hope you know how much I care*
You think you have trouble...	*You can count on me*
It's all for the best	
It's all your fault	

ABOUT A BABY

DO NOT SAY	DO SAY
She's kind of small	*My, what a beautiful baby*
Is that a birth mark?	
Were you intending to have a baby?	

IN THE CASE OF AN ADOPTION OR MULTIPLE BIRTHS

- Were you on fertility drugs?

- How long have you been trying?

- Do you know anything about the real parents?

- Why didn't they want him?

- How long did you try before you gave up?

- How long did it take for you to get her/him?

- Who does he/she look like?

- I hope he/she doesn't turn out like...

EXCUSE ME

If someone burps and they say, "Excuse me," no reply is necessary. Do not say:

- "No problem."

- "Anytime, you are forgiven."

CONCLUDING CONVERSATION

Someone calls you on the telephone and the conversation lapses:

- Response: "Well, I won't keep you."

CONCLUDING A VISIT

The proper way to say good-bye:

*   "Thank you. I had a wonderful time. Good night."

RESPONDING MODESTLY

If someone says that you and your daughter, your mom or your sister look alike, or have a striking resemblance:

*   Response: "Really? Thank you," or "Well, I'm flattered."

Hopefully, the other person to whom you are being compared will smile and say, "I'm flattered too."

❧❦❧

ATTENDING A FUNERAL

"I'm sorry about your loss," or just simply say, "I'm sorry."

IF SOMEONE IS TELLING YOU BAD NEWS

1. Just be quiet and listen. Your attentiveness shows that you are concerned.

2. You may also nod, and when you feel it's appropriate, say, "I'm sorry, this must be draining for you."

3. Do not offer unsolicited advice or express your opinion or judgement about people's character.

JOB RELATED SITUATIONS E.G. FIRINGS

1. I'm sorry you must go through this.

2. Is there anything I can do to help?

3. This must be very tough for you.

DON'T SAY

1. Things will work out for the best.

2. I told you something like this would happen.

3. What happened to someone else is even worse than what happened to you.

COMPLIMENTS & CRITICISM

This is an awkward area to deal with. Generally people receive at least one of these per day. How we handle them is another story.

CRITICISM

When delivering criticism, keep the following in mind:

- Avoid the "But", e.g., "Your dress is pretty, but..." The "But" triggers a defensive reaction. Once the person hears "But" they get busy constructing a reply instead of listening closely to further comments. Try saying, "I thought that your dress was pretty, next time, though, I would..." "Next time" does not change our initial message; "But" does.

- Keep it impersonal. Talk about behavior not personality.

- Keep it private. When criticized in public, the person is only thinking of being humiliated.

RECEIVING CRITICISM

- Accept the criticism if it is justified. Acknowledge that there is a problem. Treat it as a problem that needs to be resolved. Make it clear that you desire to fix it.

- If it's unjustified, or delivered harshly or publicly, you have every right to react. For example, you might try saying "Let's talk about this when we're both a little calmer." Or, "We need to get together and work this out, what is a good time for you?"

- If you're not sure that the criticism is justified, say, "I'm glad you're letting me know what's on your mind, I'd like to think about it and get back to you."

- If you know you messed up, simply say, "I apologize." If a little more explanation is required, then say "I never meant to offend you but I can see that I did and I am sorry."

- Don't try shifting the blame.

- It is not good manners to insult people, but if you must, do it with grace and style.

COMPLIMENTS

- These benefit the giver and the receiver. Do not allow a moment to slip by or hesitate to compliment someone because they are always well groomed or if they are consistently efficient. "You look great today" and "good job" are quite appropriate in the above case.

WHEN GIVING A COMPLIMENT REMEMBER THESE POINTS:

- Be sincere. Don't do it because you think it is a good idea. A phony compliment is easy to spot. For example if a speaker did not do well in your opinion, don't compliment them on their speech; talk about the effort they made to attend the function or their past accomplishments, if appropriate.

- Be specific. Try saying, "That boiled fish was excellent!" instead of, "You're a great cook!"

- Be unqualified. Don't put down with faint praise. e.g. "That boiled fish was pretty good."

- Don't compare. It diminishes the compliment.

WHEN RECEIVING A COMPLIMENT

- Just smile and say, "Thank you." Don't disagree or shrug off the compliment. If someone compliments your dress, don't say, "Oh, this old thing." You are really telling the other person they have poor taste. If complimented on a good job at the office, don't say, "It was nothing." This is insulting to the other person and implies that their standards are not very high. Desired response: "Thanks, I really worked hard on it."

- Don't try to upscale a compliment, e.g. "Everyone liked your hair." "Liked it? They loved it."

- Don't fail to mention others who deserve to share the compliment.

What do you say if you see an acquaintance you've not seen in a long time and their appearance has drastically changed?

- "You look marvelous." The other person may respond by saying, "Yes, weight watchers was worth my while, it really paid off." **Then** and **only then** could you engage in a conversation about dieting.

- If the person merely says, "Thank you," then talk about something else.

EMBARRASSING SITUATIONS

Someone's zipper is open or there's a run in someone's stocking or they have broccoli between their teeth. What do you do?

- Be direct but discreet.

- Get the person away from other people before you say anything, or gesture to them subtly.

- Say it in the same tone as if you were talking about the weather.

- If you don't know the person, find someone in the group who does and give them the message.

Some of us are just a little too nosey. Here again, we try to be friendly but we don't know how. I believe that if we thought more about the kinds of things we say to people and realize that we won't like it if people asked us the same question, we would be a little better off.

Most of us can attest to having something happen to us that was very embarrassing. In some instances, people told us and made it more embarrassing; in other instances we were not aware.

If you are ever caught in this situation, or if you have to tell someone something that might be embarrassing to them, be tactful.

INAPPROPRIATE QUESTIONS

- How much do you make?
- How come you don't have any children?
- Are you living together?
- How much did your outfit cost?
- Where do you live?
- What school does your children go to?
- How much are their school fees?
- How old are you?
- What's your secret?

RESPONSES TO INAPPROPRIATE QUESTIONS

- You can ignore them.

- Tell the asker that you consider the question to be rude.

- Question the asker, "Why do you ask?"

⁓ᴖᴖᴖ⁓

DEALING WITH THE DISABLED

Meeting and dealing with persons that have a disability of some kind usually causes confusion, apprehension and tension.

Many people feel uncomfortable in situations involving the disabled, partly because we are unsure of how to behave. Think about it, the disabled person on the other hand may also be uncomfortable because of the restrictions imposed on them by physical structures etc.

We must learn and be ready to react appropriately and with all the graces that we can muster so that these encounters can be a bit more pleasant.

Here are a few practical tips to assist you:

- Always offer to shake hands.

- Always speak directly to the disabled person, not through a third party. This is very important, especially if you are speaking to a hearing-impaired person.

- If you offer assistance, please wait for a response so that you will know what form the assistance should take.

- Identify yourself and others always, especially to a visually-impaired person and always let them know when you are leaving the room.

- Treat adults like adults.

- Don't shout.

- Don't touch, lean on or move a wheelchair without permission. Treat the chair as part of the person occupying it.

- When conversing with a person with a speech impediment, listen carefully and don't try to fill in a word, especially for someone with a stutter. Don't correct the pronunciation.

- Don't raise your voice. Louder is not better.

- Don't worry about phrases. Speak as you normally would.

- Focus on the person, not their disability.

- Get to know them and their interests the same way you would anyone else: by making conversation.

- Avoid using the term "handicapped." Say "disabled."

- Always say, "the person with the disability" rather than "the disabled person." Not only is it more consistent, it is more accurate.

WHEEL CHAIR ETIQUETTE

1. Keep your hands off the wheelchair unless you are asked to do so. This also applies to walkers, canes, crutches, etc.

2. If you do move them, remember to place them within sight of their owner to avoid uneasiness or panic.

3. A good time to decide to help out is when the person in the wheelchair is encountering a ramp, or a steep incline or thick carpet.

4. Respect the person's space. Avoid patting the person.

5. It's a good idea to place yourself at eye level when speaking to someone in a wheelchair. It's easier on the neck for both persons and is more comfortable.

6. If you are planning a party or a social function, consider whether the location has a wheelchair access. Remember that it may take the disabled person longer to reach the destination than others.

VISUAL IMPAIRMENT ETIQUETTE (BLIND)

Guide dogs are working animals, not pets. Do not distract them in any way while they are in a harness. If the harness is off, ask the owner if you may pet him, but do not touch him without the owner's permission.

If you are in a blind person's familiar environment, do not move things around. If you do, put them back exactly where you found them.

Here are some more tips:

• Offer assistance if you think it might be helpful, but wait for a response. If the answer is yes, offer your elbow.

• Always walk ahead of the blind person.

• Always say "step down", "step up" etc.

• When helping the person into the car, place your hand on the inside door handle, and let them go on alone.

• When entering an unfamiliar restaurant, office etc., offer your elbow and say words like "left", "right" and then place their hand on the back of the chair so that they can be seated without further assistance.

• Do not raise your voice to a blind person. It's annoying.

• When accompanying a blind person, do your best to describe the surroundings.

If You Are Meeting A Blind Person For The First Time:

1. Make your presence known right away, and if others are with you, introduce them and specify where they are, e.g. "on my left is Ray and on my right is Jonathan."

2. When offering a handshake, say something like, "allow me to shake your hand."

3.   Remember to talk to a person without sight as you would a person who can see.

4.   In a group, use the people's name as an indication to whom you are speaking.

5.   When giving money to a blind person, separate the bills into denominations and specify if they are ones, fives etc. They will identify coins by touch.

HEARING LOSS ETIQUETTE

This disability is less dramatic, but certainly more common. There are varying degrees of hearing loss, so your response needs to adjust accordingly.

•   Be sure that you have the person's attention before you begin talking. If necessary, wave a hand or tap the person gently on the shoulder.

•   Face the person you are talking to and make sure the light is on your face so that the deaf person can see your lips more clearly.

•   Don't get frustrated if you have to repeat yourself. If necessary, get someone to "sign" for you or write it down.

•   Don't repeat the same phrase over and over. Be flexible, switch words or rephrase the sentence. Some words look similar to a lip reader.

•   Some degree of expression, gestures and body language is necessary.

- Speak slowly and clearly. Don't shout and don't speak from another room.

- If a hearing-impaired person is in a group and they are laughing, explain the joke to him so that he does not feel as if they are laughing at him.

People with disabilities are very much like people without disabilities, except that their lives may require a little more courage and character than the rest of us. You will be more comfortable with them if, while acknowledging their disability, you treat them with the same respect that you expect for yourself. They don't want your pity and they deserve your admiration.

PART SIX

POSTURE

- Yours should be upright, erect and give the appearance of grace.

- You should look comfortable and never appear as if you are straining or uneasy.

- Your posture should be one that is admired.

- Your posture plays a very important part in how you carry your clothes.

- Your posture sends a message to onlookers.

- You will either give off a look of confidence or a look that you are not sure of yourself.

STANDING

- When standing, you should stand erect with one foot pivoting at an angle. You should feel comfortable; if you are, then you will appear so to others. It is important not to appear as if you are straining, or not used to standing this way.

- Your shoes should be comfortable in size and height. All of this will aid in the comfort of your posture.

- Your hands should hang loosely at your side. They should not be fidgeting with your clothes or criss-crossed in front of you. This gives the appearance of nervousness or that you lack confidence.

- Your shoulders should be erect and your chest should be slightly protruded.

- Your head should be upright and your chin up, which makes you look taller. In so doing however, do not become prideful because the Bible reminds us in I Peter 5:5 that, "God resisteth the proud and giveth grace to the humble."

- When moving around, you should have an aura of grace and excellence but your spirit should be one of humility. An "I am better than you" spirit ought not be your aim.

- Your legs should never be apart. It makes you appear slack and a little vulgar. It also draws attention to you.

WALKING

- When walking, you should walk with grace and confidence. You should be focused on knowing where you are going and just go there.

  E.g. If you walk into a room and you need to find a seat but there are no ushers, what should you do?

- You stand at the door, identify a seat in the audience and then walk straight there.

- Nothing looks more tacky than someone walking back and forth trying to find a seat.

- You should walk in a straight line, with your feet crossing over in front of each other. Don't forget to keep your shoulders erect, head straight and buttocks tucked in.

- Remember that your walk says a lot about you as a person. Sometimes your posture could be misinterpreted, but do not allow this to hinder or intimidate you from doing what you know is right.

- You should not appear to be wobbling, and your hands should hang loosely at your sides as you walk, unless you are wearing a handbag across your arm.

SITTING

People can tell a lot about you based on how you are sitting. They can tell if you are nervous, comfortable, confident, boisterous or very lady-like.

Whenever you are about to be seated after having identified where you are going to sit and then going there, you should:

- Stand in front of your seat. Ensure that you can feel the front of the seat with the back of your calves. It is important to do this so that you are confident when you actually sit down, and of course, certain that the chair is there.

- Bend your knees as you lower your bottom onto the edge of the seat. (This position allows your clothes, skirt or dress, to be in position when you sit.)

- Now, place one hand on either side of the seat a
  slide your bottom in the chair until your bottom
  touches the back of the chair.

- Your back should be erect and aligned with your
  bottom. In other words, you should not be leaning
  forward or slouching.

- Your legs can be placed in any of a number of
  positions:

    1. They can simply be placed in front of you with
        your feet together (flat-footed).

    2. They can be placed in front of you with your
        feet crossed one over the other.

    3. They can be placed to the left or right of you
        (your choice) and then crossed over.

  **NOTE: If placing to the left, then the right is
  placed behind the left ankle and vice versa.**

- When sitting, your legs should **NEVER** be apart.
  No one should be able to see your inner thighs and
  certainly not your underwear. That's also the reason
  why you should not cross your legs at the thighs.

PREPARING TO GET UP
FROM YOUR CHAIR

- When preparing to stand up, you should, again, be poised. Bring your legs to the front of you as described on the previous page.

- Slide them inward toward the chair. Use your hands as support. Place them on the seat or on your lap and push yourself up.

WALKING UP AND DOWN
STAIRS AND STEPS

When walking up a step or stairway or when coming down the same, you should not run or skip. You should turn your body slightly to the side and descend or ascend the steps sideways.

PLEASE NOTE: If you are right-handed, you should turn slightly to your left and vice versa. The reason for this is so that you have access to the full width of the steps and you lessen the chances of your heel hooking on the steps and your falling.

WHEN GETTING IN
AND OUT OF A CAR

This method works much more smoothly of course, if the car has leather seats. However, here we go:

1. Open the car door.

2. Rest your hips (buttocks) on the seat with your legs on the outside of the car and your feet on the ground.

3. Take a hold of the handle that is situated above the seat in the roof of the car or the strap, in the case of a limousine.

4. Hold firm and swing your legs in (swing in from the right if you're on the left side of the car and vice versa). i.e. lift your legs and swing them on the inside of the car, then position them on the pedal.

5. When driving, keep your thighs together down to your knees, part your legs and use your foot to release the pedals. (Different, but you could do it particularly when wearing a dress or a skirt that's short). Smile.

PART
SEVEN

TELEPHONE ETIQUETTE

1. Answer the phone no later than the second ring.

2. Say "**Hello**" as opposed to "**Hi**," then identify yourself and where you are calling from.

3. Ask, "May I Tell Him/Her Who's Calling?" as opposed to, "Who's Calling?" And be sure to tell the person.

4. Place your calls yourself when possible and try not to keep the caller waiting when the call is transferred. They will get the feeling that you think your time is more important than theirs.

5. If you get another call while you are on the phone, remember that the first call is priority. Tell the second caller you'll call him or her back.

6. When closing a call, try to end on a positive note. Always say goodbye and let the other person hang up first.

7. If you dial a wrong number, don't ask, "What number is this?" Ask instead, "Is this 457-3386?" so you can look that number up or dial more carefully the next time.

VOICE MAIL ETIQUETTE

1. Give the caller a choice, e.g. leave a message or call another number.

2. The message should always answer the 5 W's:

    Who, What, When, Where & Why.

3. Before recording your message on your voice mail, write out and practice what you are going to say.

4. Smile when you are saying it.

5. Eliminate the background music. It may be cute, but it's unprofessional.

6. Make your recording brief.

7. Leave a message even if you dialed the wrong number; e.g. say that you misdialed.

8. Give your full name.

9. Mention that you can be reached.

10. Leave your complete number.

PART EIGHT

THINGS TO CONSIDER WHEN MAKING A SPEECH

1. Determine the setting (location), i.e. Office, Conference Room or a Ballroom at a Hotel and dress accordingly. If it is an informal setting, dress up a notch from your audience.

2. What is the set-up? (i.e. podium, rows of chairs, draped table, are there panelists behind a table, etc?)

3. Based on the above, how much of you would the audience see? Dress accordingly. E.g. If you are being seen from waist up, then you would want the top half of you to be defined and strong, not droopy and lacking confidence.

4. Avoid drab colours like green/browns they give no personality.

5. What kind of microphone is being used (portable or on a stand)? Do you want to move around while you are speaking?

6. What is it that you are presenting?

7. Wear a pair of shoes with heels even if they are low, and even if you are wearing pants. They almost compel you to stand straight at the podium.

8. If your audience has full view of you, decide if you want your legs to be visible. If you decide to wear a skirt or a dress, your shoe and hosiery should make your legs look great. Sheers or skin shades stockings are best. Do not wear coloured stockings with a pattern. Sling-back pumps are always flattering.

9. Be familiar with your material so that you can connect with your audience.

10. Eye contact is very important.

11. Prepare, so that you can deal with the subject adequately.

12. Cue cards with points are excellent if you can handle it.

13. Stay within your allotted time-frame.

14. Appease your audience with a great opening, and periodically throw in a joke or story if it is suitable.

PART
NINE

ETIQUETTE FOR TRAVEL

Most of us like to travel and those of us who travel more extensively know that many times we are embarrassed because of our ignorance to habits and customs of a particular country. Remember, not everything that is acceptable in your culture means that it is appropriate in other parts of the world. Here are some tips that I hope you find useful.

1. Before boarding the plane, take some time and do some reading or watch a movie about the places you are about to visit. Learn as much as you can about the laws and customs of the country so that you can blend in as much as possible.

2. If you do not speak the language, mind your manners.

3. If you are taking a gift or sending flowers to someone, make sure that the colour and/or type is appropriate.

4. When greeting, note if it's a kiss, hug, or a handshake.

5. Respond to a handshake by matching the pressure and enthusiasm with which it's done.

6. Notice how close or how far the Natives stand from each other and follow the cultural norm.

7. Get a map of the city and see where your hotel is located.

8. Learn how to place local calls and always have coins for the use of the phone.

9. Belching and smacking in some customs are complimentary, however, leaving your mouth open when you do, is not.

WHEN TRAVELLING ALONE

- Stay at a hotel instead of a motel.

- Don't be afraid to talk to strangers.

- Be wary, however, of putting yourself in jeopardy.

- If you agree to have a meal with a stranger, do it in the hotel dining room.

- Charge the meal to your room so you don't mis-communicate the return of the date.

- Make sure the front desk personnel does not shout out your room number to the bellman. If this happens, ask for another room discreetly.

- Let the bellman check all spaces in your room to ensure that you are the ONLY person there.

- You can communicate the fact that you are not interested in getting to know someone better by giving one word answers, nodding or saying you need to take a nap.

- Check your window locks and make sure there is no other access to your room from outside.

ADDITIONAL TRAVEL TIPS

1. Make sure that your passport is valid.

2. Secure any visas that may be necessary from the appropriate Consulate.

3. Make sure that you take any vaccines / immunizations required prior to travel and ensure that they are taken in sufficient time for effectiveness. The same applies to any oral medications required. Contact your Centre for Disease Control.

4. Make sure that your Health Insurance is up to date.

5. Carry your insurance card with you.

6. Pack a mini emergency kit filled with painkillers, bandages, 'Pepto Bismol' etc.

7. Make sure to take any medications with you that you might need.

8. Check the weather conditions prior to packing.

9. Pack appropriately and as light as possible.

10. Make sure that you have all of your travel documents.

11. Take along some foreign currency if necessary for easy access. Do not travel with large sums of cash.

12. If travelling with small children, make sure that they have some form of identification at all times.

13. Be sure to pack any type of medication that they may need.

14. Purchase an adapter kit for foreign travel.

15. Get a watch that is able to show the different time zones.

16. Pack a small sewing kit.

17. Take along any extra buttons that you may have for your outfits.

18. To conquer jet lag, do not go to sleep as soon as you arrive.

19. Eat chewing gum to ease the pressure on your ear when ascending and descending.

20. Drink plenty of water when flying, as you can get very dehydrated.

21. Learn a bit about the local custom so that you are not rude and offensive.

22. Learn some basic things for the purpose of getting around, e.g. directions, ordering food etc.

23. Wear very comfortable shoes.

24. Take a little time to relax so that you do not need a vacation after the fact.

25. Have a positive attitude, be open-minded, and expect the unexpected.

26. You will always have to wait for something while travelling. When this happens, find ways to entertain yourself.

27. Do not just shop while traveling; experience the culture of the place.

28. Don't forget your camera and film.

29. Make sure that you place identification tags on all of your luggage.

30. Place all of your valuables in your carry-on bag.

31. Try to always travel with someone. It is safer and you can have more fun.

32. Make sure that the person is someone that you can share your adventure with and who has an appreciation for what you will experience.

33. Make sure you and your companion have similar travel styles.

34. You will clear customs when travelling between countries.

35. When travelling abroad, the foreign exchange rate is better once you reach your destination.

36. A travel journal is a good idea.

37. Check for the weather conditions so that you can pack appropriately.

38. Carry an empty bag or leave room in your luggage for the new stuff you will acquire.

39. To combat homesickness, carry along something that is familiar and personal e.g. a photo.

TIPS ON GREETING PEOPLE

The most important thing about an introduction is to just do it. If you don't, people around you end up feeling invisible.

- People of lesser authority are introduced to persons of greater authority.

- As you make the introduction, include a brief bit of info about those being introduced.

- How you respond is also important. Respond simply by saying, "hello" or you can add something like, "I heard you speak at---------." Keep it brief and friendly.

- You should always stand up when being introduced.

- When someone comes to visit your office, stand and come out from behind your desk unless the visitor is a coworker or someone that frequents your office.

- If it is your boss or a senior person that frequents your office, no need to stand always, but definitely stop what you're doing and give your full attention to the senior executive.

- When shaking hands (greeting) you must make eye contact.

- The handshake starts and stops briskly.

- Do not continue shaking hands through the entire introduction.

- The handshake lasts about three seconds.

- A handshake is firm but painless.

- You shake hands if someone offers his/her hand to you.

- You shake hands when you first meet someone.

- You shake hands when renewing an acquaintance.

- You shake hands when saying goodbye.

- You shake hands when greeting guests.

- You shake hands when greeting your host/hostess.

- Keep your drink in your left hand to avoid giving someone a wet, cold handshake.

Hugs and kisses are inappropriate in any business environment. Touching in the workplace is impolite even if you feel the person is your buddy (friend).

ETIQUETTE FOR ROYALTY

Most of us would never need this information, but just in case:

1. **NEVER** touch or speak to a member of the royal family first.

2. **ALWAYS** wait to be addressed.

3. Once addressed, you may curtsy or bow if you wish, **but** you must curtsy or bow to your Country's Royalty.

4. **NEVER** turn your back on royalty when exiting the room. Always back up three places and then turn.

5. **NEVER** call a member of the royal family by their name, no matter how familiar they may seem.

CONCLUSION

CONCLUSION

When people ask, as they often do, "Is etiquette still important today?" or "Is all that necessary?" I honestly reply, "Of course!" Because it has proven to be the most attractive, most practical and least objectionable way of doing things.

An acknowledgment of basic etiquette carries very definite advantages.

As always, my advice is intended to serve as a guide. It is not a restrictive set of rules but a compilation of guidelines and tools to help you.

I hope you will read the parts that apply to you; enjoy them, learn from them and find that life is more rewarding, more fun, because you have become a more confident person.

Share this information with someone, or better yet, give a copy of this book as a gift to a friend.

To contact Patrice M. Ellis write to:

Mount Tabor Full Gospel Baptist Church
P.O. Box N-9705
Nassau, N.P., Bahamas
or
pmellis@coralwave.com

For additional copies of this book, contact:

Tel: (242) 392-0708
or
Toll-free in the United States
1-700-888-FIRE (3473)

NOTES

NOTES

NOTES

NOTES

Printed in the United States
76419LV00005B/301-1500